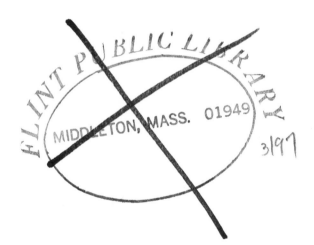

# SLOVAKIA

## *…in Pictures*

Photo © Karen L. Benson

Visual Geography Series®

# SLOVAKIA

## ...in Pictures

Prepared by
**Geography Department**

**Lerner Publications Company**
Minneapolis

Independent Picture Service

**Campers and their gear crowd a lakeside in eastern
Slovakia.**

This book is an all-new edition in the Visual Geography Series. Previous editions were published by
Sterling Publishing Company, New York City. The
text, set in 10/12 Century Textbook, is fully revised
and updated, and new photogaphs, maps, charts, and
captions have been added.

LIBRARY OF CONGRESS CATALOGING-IN-PUBLICATION DATA

**Slovakia in pictures** / prepared by Geography Dept.,
Lerner Publications Company.
    p.   cm. — (Visual geography series)
    Includes index.
    ISBN 0-8225-1912-7 (lib. bdg.)
    1. Slovakia—Juvenile literature. 2. Slovakia—
Pictorial works—Juvenile literataure. [1. Slovakia.]
I. Lerner Publications Company. Geography Dept.
II. Series: Visual geography series (Minneapolis, Minn.)
DB2712.S57 1995
943.7305′022′2—dc20                          94-45803
                                                CIP
                                                 AC

International Standard Book Number: 0-8225-1912-7
Library of Congress Catalog Card Number: 94-45803

## VISUAL GEOGRAPHY SERIES®

**Publisher**
Harry Jonas Lerner
**Senior Editor**
Mary M. Rodgers
**Editors**
Tom Streissguth
Colleen Sexton
**Photo Researcher**
Beth Johnson
**Editorial/Photo Assistant**
Marybeth Campbell
**Consultants/Contributors**
Alena Cicelova
Dana Hurtova
Anna Kozelova
Magdalena Kratochvilova
Jozef Medvecky
Stefan Zambo
Sandra K. Davis
**Designer**
Jim Simondet
**Cartographer**
Carol F. Barrett
**Indexer**
Sylvia Timian
**Production Manager**
Gary J. Hansen

Independent Picture Service

**In a wilderness area of central Slovakia, bear cubs play on
a tree branch that overhangs a river.**

**Acknowledgments**

Title page photo © John Drew 1995.

Elevation contours adapted from *The Times Atlas of
the World*, seventh comprehensive edition (New
York: Times Books, 1985).

     1  2  3  4  5  6  –  JR  –  00  99  98  97  96  95

Master Pavol (Paul), a skilled Slovak woodcarver from the town of Levoca, created this altarpiece *(detail shown)* over a period of 10 years in the fifteenth century. The tallest altar decoration in Europe, the gold-painted artwork now graces St. Jacob's Cathedral, a Roman Catholic church that is a destination for religious pilgrims.

# Contents

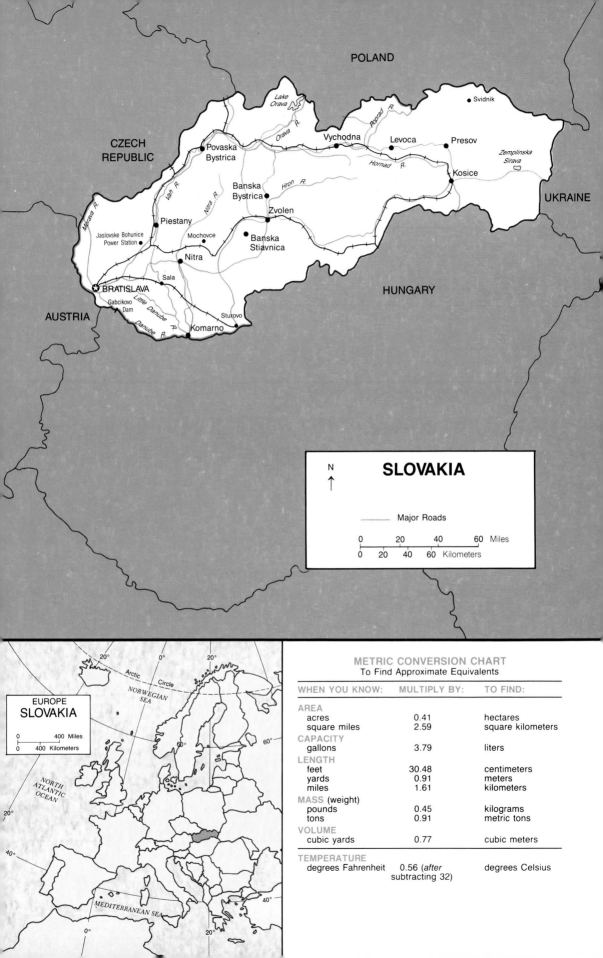

POLAND

Lake Orava

Svidnik

CZECH REPUBLIC

Orava R.

Poprad R.

Vychodna

Levoca

Presov

Povaska Bystrica

Hornad R.

Zemplinska Sirava

Kosice

UKRAINE

Vah R.

Banska Bystrica

Hron R.

Nitra R.

Zvolen

Piestany

Mochovce

Banska Stiavnica

Jaslovske Bohunice Power Station

Nitra

Sala

HUNGARY

BRATISLAVA

Gabcikovo Dam

Little Danube R.

Danube R.

Sturovo

Komarno

AUSTRIA

N

↑

**SLOVAKIA**

—— Major Roads

| 0 | 20 | 40 | 60 | Miles |

| 0 | 20 | 40 | 60 | Kilometers |

EUROPE
SLOVAKIA

0    400 Miles
0    400 Kilometers

20°   0°   20°

Arctic Circle

NORWEGIAN SEA

60°

60°

NORTH ATLANTIC OCEAN

20°

40°

MEDITERRANEAN SEA

0°   20°   40°

## METRIC CONVERSION CHART
### To Find Approximate Equivalents

| WHEN YOU KNOW: | MULTIPLY BY: | TO FIND: |
|---|---|---|
| **AREA** | | |
| acres | 0.41 | hectares |
| square miles | 2.59 | square kilometers |
| **CAPACITY** | | |
| gallons | 3.79 | liters |
| **LENGTH** | | |
| feet | 30.48 | centimeters |
| yards | 0.91 | meters |
| miles | 1.61 | kilometers |
| **MASS** (weight) | | |
| pounds | 0.45 | kilograms |
| tons | 0.91 | metric tons |
| **VOLUME** | | |
| cubic yards | 0.77 | cubic meters |
| **TEMPERATURE** | | |
| degrees Fahrenheit | 0.56 (*after* subtracting 32) | degrees Celsius |

In the early 1990s, Slovak nationalists—people who favored the establishment of a separate Slovak state—carried flags and signs that featured Slovakia's coat of arms. In January 1993, Slovakia officially became an independent country.

Photo by Archive Photos

# Introduction

The division of Czechoslovakia in early 1993 created two new nations—the Czech Republic and Slovakia. This event brought the people of Slovakia to a turning point. For the first time, Slovaks are enjoying full independence, while recovering from many years of economic stagnation and one-party rule. But they are also grappling with political turmoil and waging an intense debate over their country's future.

Before 1918 Slovakia was part of Hungary, a kingdom in central Europe. Hungarians considered Slovakia part of their ancient homeland and resisted Slovak demands for independence. The region remained mostly agricultural, with landowners controlling large estates and enjoying rights and privileges—such as voting—that were denied to farm laborers, most of whom were Slovaks.

World War I (1914–1918) brought important changes to central Europe. Hungary's defeat in that conflict allowed the Slovaks and the Czechs—who are closely related ethnic groups—to form the new Republic of Czechoslovakia. Slovakia made up nearly half of this nation.

After World War II (1939–1945), Czechoslovakia came under a new regime that was closely allied to the Soviet Union, a powerful Communist nation to the east. Communist leaders in Czechoslovakia banned private businesses and imposed strict state control over industry, agriculture, and foreign trade. The government operated the nation's information media and banned all opposition political parties.

Slovakia went through a period of rapid industrialization during the 1950s. The Communist government built immense factories in the region, and many Slovak farmers moved to the cities. Living standards improved as employment increased and as the government extended health benefits to most of the population. Nevertheless, many Slovaks still wanted self-rule. A new federation was established in 1968, with the Slovaks and the Czechs forming their own local governments.

Czechoslovakia remained under strict one-party rule until 1989. In that year, a popular revolt brought down the Communist regime. In the Czech Republic, the centralized economy was replaced by a free-market system, in which supply and demand determined wages and prices. But Slovak leaders, many of whom were former Communists, still favored a state-controlled economy. Privatization—the selling of state-owned companies to private investors—progressed much faster in the Czech Republic than it did in Slovakia.

By the mid-1990s, Slovakia had opened its economy to outside investment. Foreign as well as Slovak companies have established new, private businesses. But many factories still make outdated goods that Slovak firms have trouble selling abroad. As a result, the country's people are seeing the effects of a weak economy—high unemployment, a scarcity of some goods, and a declining standard of living.

In addition, the fall of Communism sparked turmoil among the new political parties. Slovak leaders sharply disagree on the proper pace of economic change. As a result, the government is unable to make important decisions or to agree on future policies. Slovaks are finally enjoying freedom and independence, but many citizens worry about the nation's political problems and uncertain future.

The owner of a car dealership in the western city of Povaska Bystrica answers a query from a potential customer.

Photo © Karen L. Benson

Sheep graze in a valley in the High Tatra Mountains, a range that extends along Slovakia's northern border with Poland.

# 1) The Land

Slovakia is a small, mountainous, land-locked nation in central Europe. Steep mountain ranges crisscross the country's landscape and make travel difficult. As a result, Slovakia has many areas of unspoiled wilderness, as well as villages and small towns that are only just beginning to modernize.

Slovakia covers 18,923 square miles, which makes it only slightly larger than the states of Vermont and New Hampshire combined. Slovakia's neighbors include Poland to the north, the Czech Republic to the northwest, Austria to the southwest, and Hungary to the south. Slovakia also has a very short eastern border with Ukraine, an independent nation that once was part of the Soviet Union.

## Topography

Snowcapped mountains, remote forests and pastures, winding river valleys, and fertile plains are typical of Slovakia's

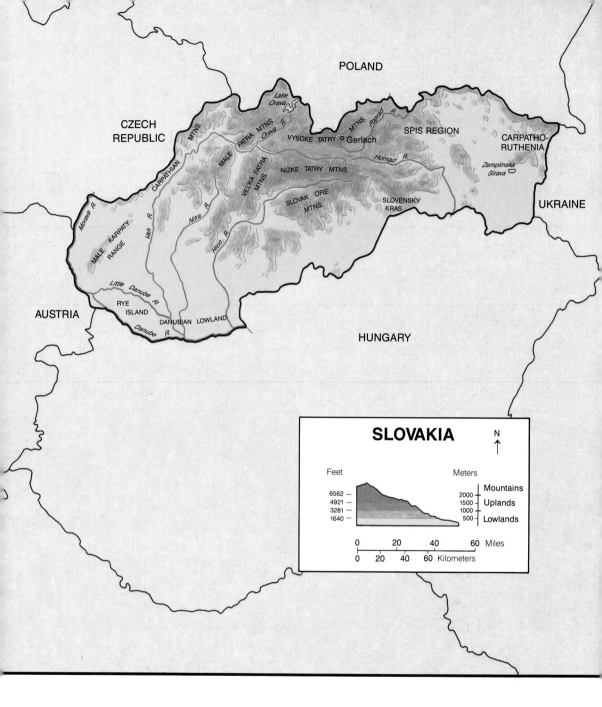

varied landscape. Lacking natural resources, level land, and fertile soil, many parts of the country have been nearly untouched by human activity over the centuries.

The rugged Carpathian Mountains stretch across central Europe in a wide arc, reaching their western limit within Slovakia. The peaks and foothills of the Carpathians roll across northern Slovakia in a series of smaller ranges that are separated by river valleys and narrow basins. Compared to Slovakia's more level southern half, the population is sparser and the climate more extreme in this part of the country.

The Male Karpaty Mountains rise near the Slovak capital of Bratislava, in the southwest, and run northward along the border with the Czech Republic. To the east are the Mala Fatra Mountains, a steep ridge divided by the Vah River. Thickly forested valleys lie between the rocky peaks, and clear mountain lakes fill small basins within the range. In large wilderness areas of the Vel'ka Fatra and Nizke Tatry ranges, hikers may spot wild boars and some rare European bears.

North of the Vah valley, and running along Slovakia's border with Poland, are the High Tatras. Ancient glaciers—slow-moving sheets of ice—carved the small freshwater lakes, sheer rock walls, and steep canyons of this range. The High Tatras include Gerlach (8,710 feet), Slovakia's highest point.

The Slovak Ore Mountains stretch across central Slovakia. After World War II, mineral deposits in this area supplied Slovak factories with raw materials and played a major role in the region's industrialization. Small towns, farms, and villages dot the river valleys, where fast-flowing streams run southward toward Hungary.

The Spis region lies east of the High Tatras and includes the upper valleys of the Poprad and Hornad rivers. The Spis towns are home to many ethnic Germans, who first emigrated to this region in the

Courtesy of Mary Ney

Farmland is scarce in rugged northern Slovakia, but some families work small plots of land near their mountain villages.

Castle ruins dominate a valley in the Spis region of northeastern Slovakia.

Photo © Mark Vasko Bigaouette

**11**

thirteenth century. To the east, along Slovakia's border with Ukraine, is Carpatho-Ruthenia, a land of rolling hills and small villages.

The lowlands of southeastern Slovakia are part of a flat, dry plain that continues into Hungary. Near the southern border is the Slovensky Kras, a limestone plateau where water erosion has carved narrow canyons and spectacular caves. An underground river runs through the 17-mile Domica Cave, one of the longest caves in the world.

The Danubian Lowland, a fertile area in southwestern Slovakia, is the country's most densely populated region. This plain stretches along the northern bank of the Danube River, which forms part of Slovakia's border with Austria and Hungary. Marshes, pastures, and fields of grains and other crops cover the landscape.

## Rivers and Lakes

Flowing between the ridges of the Carpathian Mountains, Slovakia's rivers eventually empty into the Danube River. Although only the Danube is deep enough to permit commercial shipping, other rivers provide irrigation water for farms and serve as an important attraction to boaters and tourists.

The Danube meets the Morava River just west of Bratislava. After passing the capital, the Danube divides into two channels. The main channel follows the Hungarian border, while a smaller branch, known as the Little Danube, runs directly eastward and empties into the Vah River. Between the two channels lies Rye Island. Once a hunting preserve for Slovakia's landowners and nobility, Rye Island is now home to large cooperative farms that cultivate cereal crops.

Southwestern Slovakia boasts the country's most fertile lowlands and its largest urban areas.

Rising far to the west in Germany, the Danube River twists and turns many times before passing through the Slovak capital of Bratislava. Within Slovakia the Morava, the Nitra, and the Hron rivers flow into the Danube, Europe's second longest waterway.

For many centuries, the Danube has linked the nations of central Europe and has provided a shipping route eastward to the Black Sea. In modern times, the river water has been heavily polluted by waste from factories and from the rapidly growing cities that line its banks.

The Vah River rises in the Vel'ka Fatra Mountains and runs southward through western Slovakia. At the meeting of the Vah and the Danube sits the busy port of Komarno, the site of a vast shipbuilding and ship-repair complex.

The Nitra River flows southward toward the Danube from its source on the southern slopes of the Carpathians. The Hornad River passes the city of Kosice in eastern Slovakia and then travels through the Hungarian plains to the south.

Lake Orava, in northern Slovakia, was created in 1954 by the damming of the Orava River, which follows a course parallel to the Nitra. The Liptovska Mara, another artificial lake, stretches along a plain just north of the Nizke Tatry Mountains. The Zemplinska Sirava (Slovak Sea) of eastern Slovakia attracts a large crowd of summer vacationers.

About 45 miles northeast of Bratislava, the Vah River runs through the town of Piestany. Eventually, the waterway curves southward on its route to the port of Komarno.

**13**

## Flora and Fauna

Forests cover approximately 30 percent of Slovakia's land. In central and northern Slovakia, upland pastures give way to stands of pine and spruce that cover the higher slopes of the mountains. Forests of hardy beech trees grow in the east. Reeds and marsh grasses thrive in the Danubian Lowland.

The forests of Slovakia, many of which have remained undisturbed since the region's settlement, are home to some of Europe's most varied wildlife. The High Tatras shelter many species that are rare in Europe, including brown bears, wild boars, lynxes, marmots, otters, and the chamois (a kind of antelope). Pheasants, partridges, and eagles nest in the mountains, and flocks of wild geese winter in the lowlands. Birds and mammals are protected from hunters within several national parks.

## Climate

The high mountains of western and northern Slovakia greatly affect the nation's climate. During the summer, winds from the west bring precipitation to these

Independent Picture Service

A pair of chamois (goatlike antelopes) climb a mountainside in the High Tatras. In summer the animals live in snowy areas but head for forested land during the winter months. Known for their quickness and agility, chamois usually escape hunters, who prize the animals for their valuable skins.

Photo © Mark Vasko Bigaouette

White poppies, which blanket this meadow in southern Slovakia, supply a vital oil to local cooks.

Photo © John Drew 1995

A small village nestles within the rolling hills of the Vel'ka Fatra Mountains in the north.

ranges, which shelter eastern and southern Slovakia from rain. As a result, the mountains stay cooler and wetter than the valleys and lowlands. The High Tatras, for example, get up to 70 inches of precipitation every year. Low-lying Bratislava, on the other hand, receives 26 inches annually.

Summers in Slovakia are warm, with sporadic but heavy showers. Bratislava averages 68° F in July, the hottest month, and Kosice sees average readings of 67° F. Changeable weather is common in the spring and fall, when periods of warm, dry weather may follow days of chilly winds and heavy rain.

Winters in Slovakia are usually cold and cloudy, with less precipitation than in summer. The valleys and lowlands experience high humidity, while mountainous regions stay drier and colder. Snow covers the slopes from November to April. Kosice averages 26° F in January, the coldest month, while Bratislava averages 30° F.

Occasionally, weather systems from the Mediterranean Sea, far to the south, affect Slovakia. Mediterranean winds sometimes bring hot, sunny weather to Slovakia's lowlands. Much drier winds from the vast plains of Ukraine and Russia often blow through eastern Slovakia, where temperatures are generally hotter in summer

**15**

Independent Picture Service

and colder in winter than in the rest of the country.

## Natural Resources

Slovakia was once an important mining center of Europe. Gold, copper, and iron deposits in eastern and northern Slovakia attracted thousands of immigrants, and Slovak mines poured vast riches into the treasuries of Hungarian kings and princes. But most of the historic mines have been exhausted and closed. Mining now provides employment to just 1 percent of the Slovak workforce.

The Nitra valley contains the country's richest deposits of coal, which power plants use to make electricity. Near Kosice and in southern Slovakia, miners also extract magnesite, an ingredient in steel produc-

tion. Copper and iron ore exist in the Slovensky Kras region. Limestone and gravel pits supply the construction industry. Small fields of natural gas and petroleum provide limited energy resources, and swift rivers power several hydroelectric stations. Slovakia still must import most of its energy fuels from abroad.

## Cities

Slovakia has few large urban centers and remains one of Europe's most rural nations. About 57 percent of the country's 5.3 million people are city dwellers, a lower percentage than in nearly all other European countries. Nevertheless, Slovak cities have steadily grown more crowded since the end of World War II, mainly as a result of rapid postwar industrialization.

Beneath advertisements for modern consumer goods, pedestrians make their way along a crowded sidewalk in Bratislava.

Stone buildings and winding streets *(above)* give parts of Slovakia's capital an age-old feel, while a modern park *(left)* affords residents open spaces and opportunities to enjoy recreational activities.

The Slovak capital of Bratislava (population 450,000) lies on the Danube River near Slovakia's borders with Austria and Hungary. The site of the city has been inhabited since prehistoric times and later attracted ancient settlers known as Celts. In the fifth century A.D., a Slavic group claimed the area under a leader named Braslav, who gave the city its name.

Under Hungarian rule, Bratislava was known as Pozsony. The city became the headquarters of the Hungarian Diet (parliament) in the 1500s. A bustling center of culture, education, and government, Bratislava attracted a mixed population of Slovaks, Hungarians, Gypsies, and Germans.

One of the city's most famous sites is its massive *hrad* (castle). First built in the ninth century as a fortified outlook on the Danube, the castle has burned down three times. The most recent reconstruction took place in 1953. Another famous landmark is the Cathedral of St. Martin, where many Hungarian kings were crowned.

About 10 percent of all Slovak industry takes place in Bratislava, where the most important business is chemical manufacturing. Textiles, oil refining, and food

Newlyweds and their families parade down a street in Kosice, the cultural heart of eastern Slovakia.

Photo by Andrzej Polec

processing are other key industries in the city. Bratislava ships its goods through a busy port that accommodates cargo ships and passenger vessels.

Kosice (population 230,000) is the principal city of eastern Slovakia. Founded by German settlers in the thirteenth century, Kosice later became an important cultural center. After World War II, an immense iron and steel plant was built near the city, making Kosice an important industrial hub. But the factory has also caused extensive pollution in the surrounding countryside.

Banska Bystrica (population 100,000), located on the Hron River in central Slovakia, grew rapidly after gold and other valuable metals were discovered in the area 700 years ago. German miners flocked to the town, which became one of the wealthiest in central Europe. But the mines have long been worked out, and the city now hopes to replace mining revenue with earnings from tourism.

Flowers, a fountain, and pastel-colored buildings enhance a square in Banska Bystrica. This city in central Slovakia once boasted a strong mining economy but has recently turned to tourism to make money.

Photo © Mark Vasko Bigaouette

Thousands of years ago, a massive migration of Celts entered central Europe, including Slovakia, where Celtic groups set up towns and traded goods with other peoples along the Danube.

# 2) History and Government

Humans have lived in Slovakia for at least 25,000 years. The earliest known settlements were in the Danubian Lowland, where prehistoric farmers cultivated small plots of grain. Archaeologists have also found traces of human habitation in caves in the Carpathian Mountains.

Around 1000 B.C., Celts migrated into Slovakia from the original Celtic homelands farther east. A Celtic group known as the Boii built a fortified town on the site of modern Bratislava. Here the Amber Road—which ran between the Baltic Sea

to the north and the Mediterranean Sea to the south—crossed the Danube River. From this strategic location, the Boii carried on a busy trade in finely worked metal goods, weapons, and pottery.

After settling Slovakia, as well as Bohemia and Moravia to the west, the Boii suffered invasions by large groups of Teutons. The ancestors of the modern Germans, the Teutons came from the mountains and forests along the upper Danube. The Teutonic Marcomanni defeated the Boii in 12 B.C. and occupied many of the Celtic towns in Slovakia. Meanwhile, the Franks and other Teutonic peoples moved into the Danube valley. From their fortifications along the river, the Franks staged raids on the armies of Rome, a powerful empire that held sway over southern Europe.

## Romans and Slavs

By the first century A.D., Roman legions (army divisions) had arrived on the south bank of the Danube. Unable to conquer the Teutons, the Romans built a series of strongholds along the river to mark the northern frontier of their realm.

By the fourth century, however, the sprawling empire proved too large to rule from its capital of Rome, far to the south on the Italian Peninsula. The Romans divided their territory into a western empire based in Rome and an eastern empire with its capital in Constantinople (modern Istanbul, Turkey). In both states, a Middle Eastern faith known as Christianity had been established as the official religion.

Although the Danube fortifications provided Rome with some protection, the river valley also became a convenient route for invaders from the east. In the fourth cen-

tury, Huns from the plains of central Asia stormed into central Europe. Under their leader, Attila, the Huns drove the Romans from the Danube valley. After the collapse of the Western Roman Empire in the fifth century, the Avars, another Asian people, conquered Slovakia, Bohemia, and Moravia.

Thousands of Slavs followed the Avars into central Europe in the sixth century. The Slavs poured through the narrow Carpathian passes into the plains and valleys of Slovakia. They fought with the Avars and built small, circular villages known as *okruhlice*. The Slavic peoples eventually branched out into eastern, southern, and western groups. The western Slavs included the Czechs (who settled in Bohemia and Moravia), the Poles (who lived to the north), and the Slovaks.

In 623 these groups united their forces to oust the Avars from central Europe. Slavic leaders invited Samo, a merchant who headed a strong mercenary army, to lead them. After defeating the Avars, Samo and the Slavs were attacked by the Franks. At the Battle of Vogatisburg in 637, the Slavs emerged victorious. The battle allowed Samo to establish a Slavic state

Photo by North Wind Picture Archives

**An illustration shows Roman soldiers exiting warships to conquer the peoples north of the Danube River. The Roman army's efforts failed, and, in time, the waterway marked the northernmost boundary of the Roman Empire.**

under his control, with its most powerful cities in Slovakia's Danubian Lowland. But Samo's realm quickly fell apart after his death in 658.

For two centuries after the death of Samo, Slovakia saw widespread violence and political chaos. Hostile armies crossed the region, while Slavic farms and cities declined or disappeared. Without a strong, central authority, Slavic princes ruled their small domains independently and fought with their rivals for land and power.

## The Great Moravian Empire

In the early ninth century, the Slavic prince Mojmir founded a new state in western Slovakia and Moravia. This Great Moravian Empire eventually controlled Bohemia as well as territory in what are now Poland and Hungary. Bratislava and the town of Nitra grew as political and economic centers of the empire. In 833 Prince Pribina of Nitra founded the first Christian church in the areas settled by the western Slavs.

Despite the size and growing strength of the Great Moravian Empire, its leaders greatly feared attack by the more powerful German states to the west. Many German princes and kings were practicing Christianity after being converted by missionaries from Rome, the center of the western (Roman Catholic) church. The German states were also allied with the pope, the leader of western Christianity. To resist German influence over his own state, the Moravian ruler Prince Rastislav invited missionaries from Constantinople—the center of the eastern (Orthodox) church—to convert his people to the new faith.

The brothers Cyril and Methodius arrived in 863 to bring the Slavs into the eastern church, whose rituals differed from those of the western church. These missionaries gave sermons in the Slavic language and invented a new alphabet—called Cyrillic—to transcribe Christian writings into Slavic languages. Their work hastened

Photo by Czech News Agency

The brothers Cyril *(left)* and Methodius brought Christianity to the Slovaks in the A.D. 800s. To make the Christian Gospels more accessible to the Slovak people, the missionaries invented an alphabet and translated books of the New Testament from Latin, the language of the Roman Catholic Church, into the local language.

the spread of Christianity among the Slavs of Bohemia, Moravia, and Slovakia.

But Rastislav's nephew, Svatopluk, sought to overthrow his uncle and ally with the German princes. To achieve this goal, he imprisoned Rastislav and then turned the Great Moravian Empire toward the western church. The pope sent a German bishop to Nitra, which became the religious and cultural hub of the realm. As other European peoples accepted Christianity, the western church soon became the wealthiest and most powerful institution on the continent.

## The Magyar Occupation

In the late ninth century, a huge force of Magyars from central Asia swept into Europe. The Magyars defeated the Slavs at Bratislava in 906, an event that destroyed the Great Moravian Empire. After the battle, the Magyars—the ancestors of the modern Hungarians—quickly occupied cities and towns in Slovakia, while Moravia and Bohemia allied with the leaders of Germany.

The new Hungarian rulers seized land and cities in Slovakia and controlled the region from their seat of power in the plains to the south. Slovak towns now belonged to the Hungarian king, who also had the right to revenues from the productive Slovak mines. Most Slovaks became serfs—laborers who were legally bound to the estates of landowners. Trade and mining in Slovakia benefited the king and the nobles, who treated their serfs as property.

In 1217 the rulers of Hungary granted a charter to Bratislava, allowing the city independence from the Hungarian monarchy. Enriched by tolls from traffic on the Danube River, Bratislava soon became a

In 1241 the Mongol commander Batu Khan swept into eastern Europe from previously conquered lands in Russia. After the Mongol armies destroyed farms and villages in Hungary and Slovakia, they abruptly returned to their base in the east.

Invading Magyars (ancestors of modern Hungarians) took over Slovak lands in the tenth century, adding the territory to an emerging Hungarian kingdom. Most rural Slovaks became serfs—farm laborers who could not leave the Hungarian estates to which they were legally bound.

wealthy center of commerce. But in 1241, Slovakia and much of the Danube valley suffered a devastating invasion of nomadic Mongols from eastern Asia. The Mongols burned cities and pillaged farms throughout central Europe before retreating from the region in the next year.

After the Mongol invasion, the Hungarians were determined to protect Slovakia from another attack from the east. Many landowners built fortified castles in the river valleys of central Slovakia. To strengthen the sparsely populated plains

**Hungary, A.D. 1200**

POLAND

KINGDOM OF BOHEMIA

Danube R.

BAVARIA

Vienna

DUCHY OF AUSTRIA

SLOVAKIA

Pozsony

Esztergom

Buda • Pest

KINGDOM OF HUNGARY

Mohacs

CROATIA

Belgrade

SERBIA

ITALIAN PENINSULA

Adriatic Sea

CARPATHIAN MTS.

TRANSYLVANIA

Danube River

Black Sea

N

Artwork by Laura Westlund

Marriage alliances and military conquests helped the Hungarian kingdom to expand into one of the largest realms in Europe. By the thirteenth century, the kingdom included Croatia along the Adriatic Sea, Slovakia in the north, and Transylvania in the east.

of eastern Slovakia, the Hungarian king invited Saxons from northern Germany to settle in newly built towns in this region. The kings also granted royal charters to 24 of these towns, to Kosice, and to min- ing communities in central Slovakia. The charters helped to create a strong class of wealthy merchants, artisans, and traders in the towns, which profited from mining and manufacturing.

Independent Picture Service

Landowners throughout Slovakia strengthened their defenses after the Mongol invasion. Originally built in the ninth century, Bratislava's castle was refortified to resist attack.

24

Trade along the Danube made Slovakia a valuable prize for other central European states. Otakar II, the king of Bohemia, marched his army into Slovakia and eventually extended his realm all the way to the Adriatic Sea, an arm of the Mediterranean Sea. But in 1278, Otakar died fighting Rudolph of Habsburg, the ruler of the neighboring realm of Austria. After this battle, Hungary again took control of Bratislava and western Slovakia.

Slovakia's farming estates and mines made it an important economic center of Hungary. The growing wealth of the region also enabled its landowners to become powerful enough to challenge Hungarian rule. In the early fourteenth century, the wealthy noble Mathias Cak managed to establish an independent state in Slovakia. Cak led his own army, minted his own coins from Slovak silver, and built a magnificent court. A new law code was written for the people of Slovakia, who enjoyed independence from the Hungarian kings until Cak's death in 1321.

## Protest and Invasion

In the late fourteenth century, a group of Bohemian religious leaders led by a priest named Jan Hus protested the vast power and wealth of the Catholic church. Fearing this movement, the leaders of the church captured and executed Hus in 1415. His death led to a civil and religious war in Bohemia that drove thousands of Hus's followers—called Hussites—into Slovakia. Later in the fifteenth century, Jan Jiskra, a Czech noble, invaded western Slovakia and brought Hussite ideas to the region.

Photo by Czech News Agency

During the early 1300s, the wealthy landowner Mathias Cak (above) seized control of Slovakia from the Hungarian kings. The country's independence was short lived, however, because, after Cak's death in 1321, Slovakia again fell under Hungarian rule.

Independent Picture Service

Hussites—followers of the religious reformer Jan Hus—gather in a funeral procession in Bohemia (now in the western Czech Republic) after Hus's execution in 1415. The execution sparked a civil war that drove many Hussites eastward into Slovakia.

**25**

Armies from the Ottoman Empire, which was centered in Turkey, invaded the Hungarian kingdom in the 1500s. Here, a Hungarian prince kneels to the Ottoman sultan, or ruler, Suleiman the Magnificent. To escape further Ottoman attacks, Hungarian nobles moved the Diet (the Hungarian parliament) to Bratislava. From there, they asked a member of the Austrian Habsburg dynasty (family of rulers) to act as king of Slovakia and Bohemia.

In the early sixteenth century, Hus's ideas inspired religious protests in Germany, where the priest Martin Luther broke away from Catholicism and established the Lutheran church. Followers of Luther—known as Protestants—found converts among the nobles and townspeople of Slovakia, many of whom were Hungarians and Germans. Most ethnic Slovaks living in the countryside, however, remained closely tied to the traditional beliefs of the Roman Catholic Church.

At the same time, a new threat was menacing Hungary and the rest of central Europe. Armies of Ottoman Turks had invaded from their base in Turkey and were marching up the Danube valley toward Buda, the Hungarian capital. In 1526 the Hungarian king Lajos II fought the Turks at the town of Mohacs in southern Hungary. The Turks crushed the Hungarian forces, and Lajos died while fleeing the battlefield.

The death of Lajos allowed the Turks to conquer Buda and to occupy Hungary as far north as the Danube River. Transylvania, a region in eastern Hungary, became independent. Seeking protection from the

Turks, the people of western Hungary elected Ferdinand, the ruler of Austria, as their king. A member of the powerful Habsburg dynasty (family of rulers), Ferdinand extended Habsburg control to Slovakia and to the kingdom of Bohemia.

In 1535 the Hungarian Diet, or parliament, moved from Buda to Bratislava to escape further attack by the Turks. Many Hungarian nobles also crossed the Danube to Slovakia, where they enjoyed safety, greater independence, and freedom from the heavy taxes levied by the Turkish sultan (ruler). Although they escaped conquest by the Turks, many Slovaks remained tied to the Hungarian estates as serfs.

## The Thirty Years' War

Since the time of Jan Hus, the Protestant faith had gained widespread acceptance among the nobles of Slovakia. In the early seventeenth century, Hungarian and Slovak Protestants were also struggling against the rule of the staunchly Catholic Habsburgs. In 1618 a rebellion against the Habsburgs in Prague—the capital of Bohemia—touched off the Thirty Years' War (1618–1648) between Europe's Catholic and Protestant states.

During the war, Gabor Bethlen—the Protestant ruler of Transylvania—campaigned against the Habsburgs in Slovakia. Bethlen was elected king by the Hungarian Diet in 1620, but in the next year he gave up the title and signed a treaty with the Habsburgs. Under Habsburg domination again, many of the Hungarian nobles returned to Catholic Christianity. The Treaty of Westphalia, which finally ended the Thirty Years' War, permitted the Habsburgs to regain Slovakia and to suspend the Hungarian Diet.

In the late seventeenth century, Habsburg forces defeated the Turks at Vienna, the Habsburg capital. This victory freed much of Hungary from Turkish rule but also strengthened Habsburg rule in Slovakia. German, the language of Austria, became the official language of education and government throughout Slovakia, while the Slovak language nearly disappeared. At the same time, the Habsburgs took measures to ban Protestant sects throughout the realm.

Habsburg rule sparked a violent uprising among Slovaks and Hungarians in 1703. Although the rebellion was put down, the Habsburgs did permit the Hungarian Diet to resume meeting in Bratislava. In 1711 the Habsburgs also restored the borders of the Kingdom of Hungary to those that had existed before the Turkish conquest.

Nevertheless, many ethnic Slovaks were still living in poverty and experiencing religious persecution at the hands of the Habsburg rulers. With no political rights whatsoever, Slovaks were expected to pay

Photo by MTI Interfoto

In 1620 Gabor Bethlen, a Transylvanian prince, tried to free Slovakia from Habsburg rule by having himself elected king by the Diet. Under Habsburg pressure, however, he gave up the title. In reaction to the Diet's actions, the Habsburgs suspended the Hungarian parliament.

taxes, serve in the military, and labor for the landowners. These hardships would soon prompt many Slovaks to call for self-rule within the Habsburg state.

## Habsburg Rule

Maria Theresa, who was crowned empress of the Habsburg Empire in 1740, introduced sweeping changes to the realm. Her government strengthened its control over Hungarian territory, lessened the power of the Hungarian landowners and of the Diet, and extended the use of German in Habsburg lands.

This policy of "Germanization" met resistance among Hungarian and Slovak leaders, who saw it as an attack on their nationalities. To resist the policy, the first Slovak and Hungarian newspapers were founded in Bratislava, and in 1787 the

Independent Picture Service

Maria Theresa, the Habsburg empress, inherited her throne at the age of 23. During her reign, a policy of "Germanization" attempted to strengthen Habsburg control and weaken Slovak nationalism.

Photo by North Wind Picture Archives

During the centuries of Habsburg rule, the lifestyles of rural Slovaks changed very little. The people still inhabited rough dwellings, worked for low—if any—wages, and had no political rights.

In 1848 Slovak nationalists met with other Slavic activists in Prague *(right),* the capital of Bohemia, to discuss self-rule and civil liberty. The Slovaks wanted to set up a federation with the Czechs, who lived in Bohemia, but the Habsburgs disregarded the idea.

Catholic priest Anton Bernolak published the first Slovak grammar book. To replace Latin—the ancient language of Rome that church leaders still used—Bernolak developed a literary language that many Slovak religious leaders adopted in their writings.

In the early nineteenth century, the Habsburg lands came under attack by the armies of Napoleon Bonaparte, the leader of France. In 1805 Napoleon defeated the Habsburg forces at the Battle of Austerlitz in Moravia. But Napoleon was driven from Europe for the last time in 1815, and postwar treaties strengthened Austria's hold over Hungary, Slovakia, Ruthenia, and the Czech lands. Habsburg rulers also controlled local parliaments, including the Hungarian Diet, and had the power to revoke any decision made by these bodies.

## Nationalist Revolts

By the middle of the nineteenth century, the many Slavic peoples living under Habsburg rule were demanding greater liberty. Although some Slavic leaders wanted to stay within the Austrian Empire, others sought full independence from the Habsburgs. In Slovakia attempts by the Hungarians to force schools and churches to use the Hungarian language caused increasing anger among the ethnic Slovaks.

In 1848, as popular rebellions swept through the capitals of Europe, a Slavic Congress took place in Prague, the capital of Bohemia. Slovak representatives at the congress sought to form a Czech and Slovak federation within the Austrian Empire. But the Habsburgs denounced the congress and ignored its demands.

In the same year, Ludovit Stur, a Slovak member of the Hungarian Diet, founded a Slovak National Council with other Slovak nationalists. The council petitioned the Diet for the right to form local Slovak assemblies and to use the Slovak language in the schools. But Hungarian politicians, who saw Slovakia as Hungarian territory, strongly opposed these measures. When the Diet rejected the Slovak petitions, fighting broke out in Slovakia. Hungarian forces soon put down the uprising and executed several rebel leaders.

**29**

At the same time, ethnic Hungarians were staging their own nationalist revolt against the Habsburgs. This rebellion was crushed by the armies of Austria and Russia, a powerful Slavic empire to the east that had allied with the Habsburgs. For the next 20 years, the Habsburgs kept firm control of their empire and ignored demands for independence from Slovaks and Hungarians.

## Austria-Hungary and Slovakia

During the 1860s, Austria suffered military defeats in Italy and in Prussia, a kingdom in northern Germany. Continuing rebellion among the Slavs and Hungarians was also weakening the realm. In 1867, to keep Austria from breaking apart, the Habsburg emperor Franz Joseph agreed to the formation of a new state known as Austria-Hungary. By this compromise, Hungary won a completely independent parliament as well as its own administrative and judicial system.

But this action also dashed any hopes for freedom the Slovaks had. Determined to keep Slovakia under their control, Hungarian leaders started a campaign of "Magyarization," named after the nation's ancestors. Hungarian became the only official language in Slovakia, and all Slovak schools in the region were closed.

This policy and the continuing poverty of their homeland drove thousands of Slovaks to emigrate. Those who remained made up a discontented class of farmers and factory workers. Slovak nationalism grew among these laborers throughout the late 1800s, leading to the formation of the Slovak National party. The party allied with Russia, which supported independence for the Slavic peoples living in Austria-Hungary.

## The New Republic

In the early 1900s, turmoil spread among the Slavic peoples of Austria-Hungary. In 1914 the Habsburg heir was assassinated by an ethnic Serb. War soon erupted between Austria and Serbia, an independent Slavic nation. Germany allied with Austria-Hungary, while Russia supported Serbia. Britain, France, and Italy joined forces against Germany, setting the stage for World War I (1914–1918).

Although they were still subjects of the Habsburgs, the Czechs and the Slovaks opposed fighting against their fellow Slavs (the Russians and Serbians). Many Slovaks deserted the Austrian army to form a Czechoslovak Legion. This unit fought alongside the Russians until 1917, when revolutionaries known as Communists overthrew the Russian government and forced Russia out of the conflict.

During the war, the Czech nationalists Tomas Masaryk and Eduard Benes fled to Britain, where they set up a Czechoslovak National Council with the Slovak leader

Courtesy of Library of Congress

In the early twentieth century, the Slovak nationalist Milan Stefanik resurrected the idea of a Czech and Slovak federation. He worked with Czech leaders to establish this new state, in which he envisioned Slovaks ruling themselves.

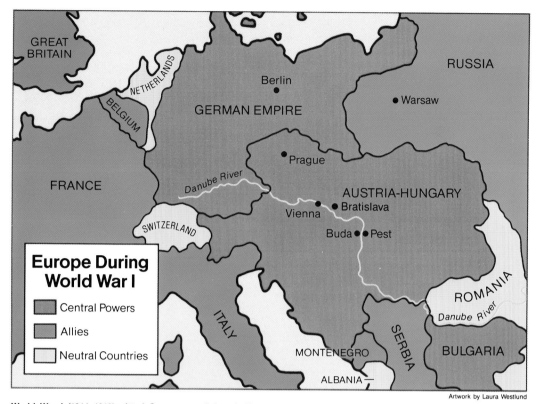

World War I (1914–1918) pitted Germany and Austria-Hungary (the former Habsburg Empire) against Russia, France, Britain, and Italy. The defeat of Austria-Hungary led to the breakup of Habsburg lands, including Slovakia and Bohemia. These two areas, along with Moravia and Ruthenia, combined in 1918 to form Czechoslovakia. Despite prewar discussions with Stefanik, Czech leaders offered Slovaks few governmental positions within the new nation.

Milan Stefanik. In 1916 the council laid plans for an independent federation of the Czechs and Slovaks. Two years later, in the United States, Masaryk signed the Pittsburgh Convention, a document that called for an independent Czech and Slovak state. Masaryk pledged that the Slovaks would rule themselves independently within this federation.

In the fall of 1918, as Germany and Austria-Hungary suffered defeat on the battlefield, the Czechoslovak National Council moved to Prague. In October this body declared the founding of Czechoslovakia, a new republic that included Slovakia, Ruthenia, Moravia, and Bohemia. (In 1920, under the Treaty of Trianon, Hungary would officially give up its claims to Slovak territory).

The war ended in November 1918, when Germany surrendered and the Habsburg emperor abdicated (gave up) his throne. The empire collapsed, and Hungary won its independence. The victorious allies set down severe terms of surrender to Germany and Austria, both of which were forced to give up territory and to make war reparations (payments). At the same time, a civil war was raging in Russia between Communists and supporters of the Russian monarchy. Eventually, the Communists prevailed and established the Soviet Union, a state that included Russia, Ukraine, and several other republics.

Czechoslovakia's National Assembly—which included 58 Slovak representatives—elected Tomas Masaryk president of the new nation. Despite Masaryk's promises during the war, the Slovaks enjoyed little independence in the new state. Instead, the assembly and its Czech leaders sought to strengthen the central government, which was dominated by ethnic Czechs. In addition, Czech officials took many of the high administrative posts within Slovakia. Although the government allowed a separate Slovak legislature to meet during the 1920s, this body had little power.

Feeling betrayed, many Slovaks continued to press for a nation of their own. Their demands gave rise to a Slovak nationalist movement led by Andrej Hlinka, a Slovak Catholic priest. After founding the Slovak People's party, Hlinka was elected to the National Assembly, where he campaigned for Slovak independence. Although his efforts were unsuccessful, the People's party would become the most active political group in Slovakia.

## Hlinka and Tiso

Economic and social turmoil in postwar Germany led to the rise of the Nazi party under Adolf Hitler. Blaming Jews, Communists, and the allies' harsh terms of surrender for Germany's problems, Hitler

Photo by Bettmann Newsphotos

Born in 1864, Father Andrej Hlinka had been imprisoned by the Habsburgs for leading Slovak nationalist activities in the early twentieth century. Founder of the Slovak People's party, he opposed unification with the Czechs and pressed for Slovak self-rule within Czechoslovakia throughout his life. In the late 1930s, just before his death, Hlinka supported closer ties with Germany, which was rearming after its defeat in World War I.

vowed to avenge his nation's defeat in World War I and to establish an empire of ethnic Germans in central Europe.

Photo by UPI/Bettmann

Jozef Tiso (right), who followed Hlinka as head of the Slovak People's party, openly connected his political group with Germany's Nazi party. Here, he shakes hands with a Nazi official during a visit to Austria, which was also part of the Nazi alliance. In 1939, after German troops occupied Bohemia and Moravia (the latter now the eastern Czech Republic), Tiso formed a Slovak government that took its orders from Germany.

Meanwhile, a group of fervent nationalists seized control of the Slovak People's party and set up a paramilitary unit called the Hlinka Guards. This group demanded separation from Czechoslovakia and closer ties with Germany and with Italy, whose leader had allied with Hitler. After Hlinka's death in 1938, the Hlinka Guards and their supporters became a powerful faction within Slovakia.

At this time, Hitler was demanding the surrender of all territory in Czechoslovakia that held a majority of ethnic Germans. Seeking to avoid another world war, several European leaders signed an agreement in September 1938, giving in to Hitler's demands. Too weak to resist Hitler's powerful armies, Czechoslovakia lost more than one-third of its territory. One month later, Hungary—which was allied with Germany—occupied southern Slovakia, where most of Slovakia's ethnic Hungarians lived.

In March 1939, Hitler invaded the rest of Bohemia and Moravia. Jozef Tiso, Hlinka's successor as the head of the Slovak People's party, then formed a Slovak government closely allied with Germany and the Nazi party.

Germany's attack on Poland in September 1939 led to World War II (1939–1945). During the war, German troops occupied Slovakia. Factories in the region made weapons and ammunition for the German armies, and Slovaks formed military units to fight alongside Germany's forces. The Slovak government also allowed Germany to deport thousands of Slovak Jews to concentration camps, where many of the prisoners were murdered.

After defeating Poland and occupying much of central Europe, Hitler ordered a full-scale invasion of the Soviet Union in 1942. But as the war progressed, the tide of battle turned against Germany. Slovak units within the German armies mutinied, while a resistance movement formed against the Tiso government. An uprising against German occupation that erupted in Slovakia in August 1944 took Hitler's forces two months to suppress.

Meanwhile, Soviet armies were advancing rapidly into central Europe. In October 1944, the Soviet Union occupied and annexed (took over) Ruthenia. Soviet forces were stationed in Slovakia and in most of Bohemia and Moravia by May 1945, when Germany surrendered.

Using low bushes as cover, Slovak rebels fought against the Nazis in 1944, just as World War II (1939–1945) was drawing to a close.

Independent Picture Service

## The Communist Regime

The end of the war saw the revival of a united Czechoslovakia (except for Ruthenia, which became part of Ukraine). With Soviet forces occupying the country, Klement Gottwald—the leader of the Czechoslovak Communist party—headed a new coalition government as prime minister, with Eduard Benes as the president. A Slovak National Council was set up as the new legislature of Slovakia, although this body had limited lawmaking powers. Most decisions were made at the national, rather than regional, level.

In the chaotic postwar years, the Communists gained popularity among many factory and farm laborers. This enabled Gottwald to appoint his colleagues to several powerful government posts. The party gradually forced non-Communists out of the government and nationalized (seized from private owners) large Czech and Slovak industries. In late 1947, the Slovak Communist party, led by Gustav Husak, took control of the Slovak National Council. By February 1948, Communists made up a majority in the National Assembly and in the Czechoslovak government.

Opposed to the regime, Benes resigned the presidency and was replaced by Gottwald. The Communists ran the Czechoslovak media and jailed or executed their opponents—many of whom were Slovak nationalists. Husak himself was jailed for supporting Slovak independence.

Czechoslovakia's government—as well as the new Communist governments of Poland and Hungary—allied closely with the Soviet Union. Soviet leaders formed the Warsaw Pact, a military alliance of Communist nations in central Europe. Working from the Soviet economic model, the new Czechoslovak regime banned private ownership of large businesses and farms. A series of five-year plans set production goals for Czech and Slovak industries and fixed wages and prices.

Within Slovakia, the government forced private farmers to join state farms and

Independent Picture Service

In postwar Czechoslovakia, a new government eventually took power and allied itself closely with the Communist regime in the Soviet Union (formerly Russia). Czech and Slovak leaders focused on expanding Czechoslovakia's industrial sector. This factory in Sala, just east of Bratislava, produced farm fertilizers.

cooperatives. This policy of "collectivization" placed all crop growing and marketing under government control. The Communists also developed heavy industries, including steelmaking, metal refining, and the production of machinery and weapons. Manufacturing replaced agriculture as Slovakia's principal economic activity, and a growing percentage of Slovak laborers worked in urban factories.

During the 1950s, under President Antonin Novotny, the economy of Czechoslovakia grew rapidly, even though the government banned most trade with non-Communist countries in western Europe. But central planning also caused inefficiency. With limited foreign trade, the government gained little outside investment for new plants and machinery. Czechoslovak factories gradually grew obsolete, and their fixed wages gave workers no incentive to increase their productivity.

By the 1960s, the nation's economy was stagnant. Factories and farms could not meet production quotas set by the government, and many Slovak workers saw their standard of living begin to decline. Shortages of food and consumer goods caused growing opposition to the government, which still allowed no criticism of its policies in the state-controlled media. Members of the Communist party began pressing for economic changes and political reform. At the same time, many Slovak Communist leaders were demanding a semi-independent Slovak republic.

## Reform and Invasion

The reform movement gathered strength in the mid-1960s. Alexander Dubcek, a pro-reform member of the Slovak Communist party, emerged as Novotny's leading opponent. Dubcek favored some private ownership of small businesses, a lifting of controls on the media, and the establishment of a federal state that would include separate Czech and Slovak republics.

Fearing the Soviet reaction to such changes, Novotny harshly criticized Dubcek and resisted the reform movement. Nevertheless, most members of the Communist party saw Dubcek's ideas as a solution to the nation's worsening economic problems. In January 1968, party members elected Dubcek secretary-general (head) of the Czechoslovak Communist party. This position made him the leader of the government, and two months later Novotny resigned the presidency.

Under Dubcek the party lifted state control of the media, proposed democratic elections, and prepared to end wage, price, and production controls. The state also planned to reform its central-planning system. These actions greatly alarmed other leaders within the Warsaw Pact, who feared the loss of their power if their own citizens demanded such changes.

On August 20, the Soviet Union and several of its allies invaded Czechoslovakia. The Soviets arrested Dubcek and other pro-reform leaders. Warsaw Pact forces occupied Czechoslovakia, and a strict Communist regime replaced Dubcek's government.

The new government sought to meet opposition within Slovakia by granting further self-rule to the region. In the fall of 1968, Czechoslovakia became a federation made up of separate Czech and Slovak republics. Each republic had its own legislature, prime minister, and administration. To improve economic conditions within Slovakia, the regime also invested more money in Slovak industries.

In the next year, Gustav Husak became the new head of the Czechoslovak Communist party. Under Husak the party ousted many leaders who had supported Dubcek's reforms. The regime also arrested its opponents and sent them to work in factories and on collective farms. Czechoslovakia returned to strict central planning and to wage and price controls.

Photo by UPI/Bettmann

In 1968, angry citizens stormed a Soviet tank on a street in Bratislava. The armored vehicle was part of the Soviet Union's attempt to halt an economic reform movement that President Alexander Dubcek, a Slovak, had been spearheading in Czechoslovakia.

**Gustav Husak** *(above)*, who disagreed with Dubcek's reforms, succeeded him in power. Husak controlled the nation's economy, establishing fixed prices, wages, and production quotas. At the same time, in answer to Slovak demands for more self-rule, the country became a federation of separate Czech and Slovak republics. Each of the two members of the federation had its own parliament, its own prime minister, and its own bureaucracy.

## Growing Opposition

Husak's government was unable to revive the Czechoslovak economy, however. Opposition grew among the nation's writers, artists, and musicians, who fought against the strict censorship of their works. In 1977 many of these opponents drew up and signed a document—called Charter 77—demanding an end to censorship and to state control of the media. The document became a rallying point for those demanding open elections and a multiparty state.

Although the Husak regime kept a tight rein on the country's economy, reformers were soon making gains in the Soviet Union. In the mid-1980s, the Soviet president Mikhail Gorbachev allowed some private businesses to operate and loosened his government's control of the Soviet media. The changes also affected the countries of the Warsaw Pact, whose Communist leaders were facing growing demands for similar reforms.

The end of Communist control in Czechoslovakia came swiftly in the fall of 1989, when antigovernment demonstrations in Prague prompted Husak to resign his post. The Czech writer Vaclav Havel, a signer of Charter 77 and a popular opposition leader, was then named as the new president. Non-Communist political parties emerged to campaign for office. Elections in the summer of 1990 brought Public Against Violence, a Slovak opposition movement, to power in the National Assembly. Vladimir Meciar, one of the movement's leaders, became the Slovak prime minister.

## Recent Events

Czechoslovakia's new leaders prepared to replace the country's state-controlled economy with a free-market system. The

Vladimir Meciar became prime minister of the Slovak republic in 1990, soon after Czechoslovakia rejected Communism and forced Husak to resign. Meciar strongly opposed the economic reforms being considered by Czechoslovakia's legislature and pressed Slovakia to separate completely from the Czech republic—a change that occurred in 1993. Since then, Meciar's Movement for a Democratic Slovakia has experienced internal problems, as well as opposition from other Slovak political parties.

Artwork by Laura Westlund

After gaining full independence in January 1993, Slovaks flew the new nation's official emblem. It shares the white, blue, and red colors that appear on flags of other Slavic countries, such as the Czech Republic, Russia, and Slovenia. The Slovak coat of arms, however, features a design that originated in Hungary.

government sold businesses to private owners and dropped controls over production, prices, and wages. But this program ran into opposition from many Slovak politicians, who feared that privatization would cause widespread unemployment and inflation (rising prices).

An aggressive and outspoken leader, Meciar opposed privatization and sought Slovakia's complete independence. These opinions earned him many enemies within the Slovak National Council, which voted to remove Meciar from his post in March 1991. Meciar then founded the Movement for a Democratic Slovakia (MDS). In the national elections of June 1992, the MDS won a majority of seats in the Slovak legislature, and Meciar returned as Slovakia's prime minister.

The privatization of companies in Bohemia and Moravia moved ahead quickly, but many Slovaks supported Meciar's opposition to free-market reforms. The debate between Czechs and Slovaks grew increasingly bitter as legislators found themselves unable to agree on the terms of a new constitution. As a result, in September 1992, Slovakia adopted its own constitution. Later that fall, the National Assembly agreed to split Czechoslovakia into two separate countries. In January 1993, Slovakia officially became independent, while Bohemia and Moravia combined to form the new Czech Republic.

During the early 1990s, the transition to a free market brought hardship for many Slovak workers who lost their jobs as the country's many obsolete factories closed.

Yet foreign companies in search of an inexpensive labor force have invested in Slovakia's factories and businesses. By the mid-1990s, the nation was expanding its trade with western Europe and enjoying rapid economic growth.

## Government

The constitution of Slovakia was officially adopted on January 1, 1993, when Czechoslovakia was formally divided. The National Council of the Slovak Republic—the Slovak legislature—includes 150 representatives, who are elected to four-year terms. The council passes laws and amendments (changes) to the constitution. Members also have the power to elect the nation's judges and the president.

Slovakia's president serves a five-year term but may be elected to only two consecutive terms. The president negotiates treaties, signs laws, and declares a referendum (public vote) on important issues. The president also names the prime minister, who is usually the leader of the party holding the most seats in the legislature. On the recommendation of the prime minister, the president appoints the deputy prime ministers and the heads of Slovakia's 14 ministries.

The highest court in Slovakia is the supreme court. District courts and county courts hear cases at the local level, while a constitutional court decides important questions of law and rules on whether or not new laws passed by the legislature contradict the constitution.

Administratively Slovakia is divided into four regions, one of which includes Bratislava. The country also has 38 smaller districts known as *okresy*.

Photo © Luke Golobitsh

**Slovakia has opened up its economy and, as a result, has more billboards that advertise products made in the United States and Europe.**

The National Council—the Slovak parliament—meets in Bratislava. Individual parties have had trouble maintaining a majority of seats in the legislature, so most governments have been led by coalitions, or combinations, of parties.

Signs at border crossings show off Slovakia's new status as an independent republic.

Hikers rest on the slopes of the High Tatras.

# 3) The People

Despite its rapid industrialization after World War II, Slovakia remains one of central Europe's most rural nations. Of the nation's 5.3 million inhabitants, 43 percent live in rural areas. The lowlands of the southwest are Slovakia's most densely populated region. The High Tatras and Carpatho-Ruthenia hold the fewest people per square mile. Overall, Slovakia's population density stands at 284 persons per square mile.

## Ethnic Groups

Slovakia has been settled by several different ethnic groups during its long history. Ethnic Slovaks, who make up 86 percent of the population, arrived in the fifth century during the migration of the Slavs into central Europe. Although they are both Slavic peoples, Czechs and Slovaks have developed entirely separate cultures. Slovakia's language, writing, music, and food all differ from those of the Czechs.

Hungary's control over Slovakia ended after World War I, but conflict still exists between Slovaks and ethnic Hungarians, who account for 11 percent of Slovakia's population. Most of these Hungarians live in southern Slovakia and make up a majority in areas near the Danube River and the Hungarian border.

Descendants of the Magyars, ethnic Hungarians in Slovakia speak Hungarian and send their children to Hungarian schools. Many Hungarians are also seeking more independence from the Slovak government. Some of Hungary's leaders have shown sympathy toward these demands, and the issue has led to increasing tension between the governments of Slovakia and Hungary.

Eastern Slovakia is the home of the Rusyn people, who live in small and scattered rural villages. The Rusyns speak a dialect of Ukrainian and are related to the ethnic Ukrainians who live to the east. Gypsies, a people who may have originated in southern Asia, dwell mostly on the outskirts of Slovak cities and towns. Also known as Romanies, Gypsies form 1.5 percent of the population. Their nomadic way of life has isolated them from the rest of Slovak society. As a result, they suffer high unemployment and the nation's lowest living standards.

**Wearing traditional clothing in preparation for a festival, a pair of ethnic Slovaks enjoy a private joke.**

(Right) An elderly woman of the Rusyn ethnic group lives in eastern Slovakia, a region that has historic ties to Ukraine. (Below) After decades of forced integration into Slovak society, Slovakia's Gypsies (also called Romanies) have begun to organize into political groups and have won some local and national elections. These young Gypsy girls make their home near Presov, a large town in the central eastern section of the country.

Photo © Karen L. Benson

Photo © Karen L. Benson

During religious festivals, Slovak Roman Catholics wear traditional costumes to services.

## Religion

After World War II, the new Communist government of Czechoslovakia saw the nation's churches as a strong rival for the loyalty of Czech and Slovak citizens. The state exiled or imprisoned religious leaders, placed strict limits on public religious worship, and forced many churches to close.

The government also banned private religious schools.

The fall of the Communist government in 1989 ended these restrictions. Churches were restored, and some religious schools reopened. Slovaks, who are mostly Roman Catholic, returned to worship in great numbers.

**43**

Slovakia is home to many other branches of the Christian faith. Orthodox Christians follow the teachings of the eastern church, which originated in Constantinople and later split from Roman Catholicism. Protestant churches include the Evangelical Church, the Reformed Church, and the Baptist Church.

The Rusyns of eastern Slovakia belong to the Uniate Church, which formed in the late sixteenth century. A branch of the Roman Catholic Church, the Uniate sect is loyal to the Catholic pope but uses Orthodox rituals and texts during its services. Slovakia also has a small Jewish community of a few thousand members.

During World War II, Jews in Slovakia were deported from Bratislava and other towns to concentration camps in Germany and Poland.

## Health and Education

After the division of the Czech Republic and Slovakia in 1993, the two nations adopted different social-welfare policies. Czech officials now allow private health insurance companies to operate, but the Slovak government still controls most health insurance through public agencies. Employers and workers make regular contributions to this system.

Old churches and commercial buildings dominate the landscape of Banska Stiavnica, a town that made its mark in the 1700s as a silver mining hub.

While many of its neighbors are experiencing negative or zero population growth, Slovakia has an annual growth rate of 0.4 percent—one of the fastest in central Europe. If this rate continues, the country's population will double in 182 years. In addition, 25 percent of Slovakia's population is younger than 15 years. This is a high figure for any European nation and means the country's population growth rate will probably continue to increase.

By many important health standards, however, Slovakia lags behind its neighbors. Infant mortality—the number of infants that die before age one—is high at 16 deaths out of every 1,000 births. The ratio of hospital beds and doctors to the population is lower than in the Czech Republic. Life expectancy for Slovaks born in the mid-1990s stands at 71 years, about average for central Europe.

Many Slovak children begin their schooling at age three, when they attend a *materska skola,* or preschool. At age six they enter the *zakladna skola,* an eight-year elementary school. Students may then continue at a secondary school, but the government does not require secondary education. Since the fall of the Communist government, private schools have also been allowed to operate.

Secondary institutions in Slovakia include grammar schools (*gymnazium*), which prepare students for higher education. Vocational schools train students for future careers in industry and business. Slovakia has 14 institutions of higher education, including Komensky University and the Academy of Fine Arts in Bratislava. But since the breakup of Czechoslovakia, the government has reduced its support of these schools, forcing students to pay a larger share of their tuition.

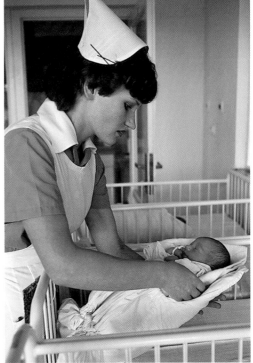

A nurse in the eastern town of Svidnik lays a newborn down for a nap. Slovakia has one of the fastest growing populations among nations in central Europe.

One out of every four Slovaks is younger than 15 years of age.

Signs in Slovak, Ukrainian, and German reflect the many languages spoken in Slovakia.

## Language and Literature

Slovak is a member of the West Slavic family of languages, a group that also includes Polish and Czech. Slovak and Czech have many words in common, although certain letters and sounds are unique to each language. Although they may speak one of many local dialects, Slovaks and Czechs can easily understand one another.

Slovakia's various ethnic minorities speak their own languages in addition to Slovak. Hungarian, a Finno-Ugric language that is unrelated to the Slavic tongues, is the first language of many ethnic Hungarians living in southern and eastern Slovakia. Rusyns use a Slavic dialect related to Ukrainian, and Gypsies speak Romany. Most ethnic Poles and Germans can speak the language of their ancestors in addition to Slovak.

Before the nineteenth century, Slovak was only a spoken language, and Slovak authors used Latin, Hungarian, or Czech in their writings. The Slovak clergyman Jan Kollar produced *The Daughter of Slava*, a collection of sonnets in the Czech language, in 1824. During the 1840s, Ludovit Stur developed *sturovcina*, a new Slovak literary language. But Hungarian rule prevented many Slovak writers and poets of the time from publishing their works in any language.

Slovak literature thrived after the founding of Czechoslovakia in 1918. Stefan Zary and other Slovak poets of the 1920s often used unusual symbols and dreamlike images in their works. Zary's most famous collection of verse was *The Wandering Spider*. Martin Kukucin, known as the father of Slovak realism, described everyday life in *Mother Calls*, in *The House on the Slope*, and in many short stories.

World War II and the rise of Communism became important subjects for postwar Slovak writers. Czechoslovakia's Com-

The writer Ladislav Mnacko left Slovakia in the late 1960s so he could have the freedom to criticize the Communist regime, particularly on its policies regarding the Middle East. In response, the government of Czechoslovakia took away Mnacko's citizenship and expelled him from the Communist party.

munist government required novelists to glorify the achievements of peasants, factory laborers, war heroes, and the new regime. In *Kronika,* for example, Peter Jilemnicky praised Communist guerrillas who fought during the Slovak uprising of 1944. *The Fallow Field* was Jilemnicky's tribute to the Slovak peasantry.

But Communism also had its critics. Dominik Tatarka denounced Communist policies in *The Demon of Consent.* Ladislav Mnacko, who fled Czechoslovakia after the Soviet invasion of 1968, described the event in *The Seventh Night* and the corruption of Communist officials in *The Taste of Power.* Mnacko gained a large audience with his straightforward, journalistic style.

Members of the Slovak underground assemble at a rallying point during the uprising of 1944. In the book *Kronika,* Peter Jilemnicky recounted the rebellion of Communist guerrillas and other Slovaks against the Nazi occupation and the pro-German Tiso government. The revolt lasted two months and hastened Germany's defeat in World War II by forcing the Nazis to use scarce military resources.

**47**

In Vychodna, northern Slovakia, Slovak musicians *(left)* perform traditional tunes for an audience at an annual folk festival, while dancers *(below)* twirl and sway at a street fair.

Photo © John Eastcott/Yva Momatiuk

## Music

Slovakia has one of central Europe's richest folk music traditions. Hundreds of years ago, the *igric,* a singer of epic tales, entertained in poor villages as well as at royal courts. Slovak musicians wrote folk melodies that were passed down from one generation to the next. Immigrants from Romania, Germany, and Hungary have also brought their music to Slovakia.

In more recent times, composers such as the Czech Leos Janacek and the Hungar-

Photo © Mark Vasko Bigaouette

48

Small ensembles, such as this duo of harpist and flutist, play both classical music and Slovak folk songs.

ian Bela Bartok collected Slovak folk songs and often incorporated them into their own works. In the process, these composers discovered several principal Slovak song styles. The "pastoral (rural) style," which was common among highland dwellers in the north and west, included bandit songs and shepherd songs. The "country style" of the fertile agricultural plains and snaking river valleys featured wedding songs and harvest songs.

Modern folk songs tell of the emigration of Slovaks to foreign nations before World War I and of the Slovak uprising of 1944. Under Communism, popular music became a means of supporting Communist ideals. During the 1950s, songwriters used traditional melodies to praise industrialization and the new collective farming system. In all, more than 16,000 Slovak folk songs have been published.

A variety of instruments accompany Slovak songs and dances. There are more than 100 kinds of flutes, including the *fujara*, which is almost six feet long. The *fanforka* is a reed instrument similar to a clarinet, and the *gajdy* is a set of bagpipes. Violins and other stringed instruments often perform together in small groups along with the *cymbal* (dulcimer), a hammered string instrument.

## Food

Slovaks prepare a wide variety of traditional foods, and the nation's farms, lakes, and forests provide plenty of fruit, vegetables, fish, and meat. One of the most popular dishes is a plate of traditional *bryndzove halusky* noodles, which are made from potatoes, flour, water, eggs, and salt, then boiled and served with fried bacon and sheep's cheese. Slovaks also enjoy *kapustnica,* a hearty cabbage soup. Wild game such as roast goose, venison, pheasant, rabbit, and fresh fish—often trout or carp—also appears on Slovak tables.

Slovakia's cuisine shows the influence of neighboring countries. From Hungary came goulash—a stew flavored with garlic, onions, and paprika—and *cikos token,* a spicy mixture of onions, peppers, and pork. Slovak cooks also prepare traditional fare from Vienna, including noodles, pancakes, and pastries.

Many Slovak adults enjoy dry white wine from vineyards in the Male Karpaty region and near Hungary. *Slivovica* is a sweet plum brandy served before a meal. Cafes in Bratislava and other cities offer *presso,* or strong espresso coffee.

## Recreation and Sports

The rugged mountain ranges of Slovakia offer many opportunities for outdoor sports. Alpine (downhill) skiers flock to several resorts in the Nizke Tatry and in other mountain ranges. The nation has applied to the International Olympic Committee for the opportunity to host a future winter Olympic Games.

Photo by Robert L. and Diane Wolf

Inherited from Hungary, goulash is a popular entree in Slovakia. The thick stew contains potatoes, green peppers, at least two kinds of meat, paprika, and other spices. A nonmeat dish or dessert often follows a serving of goulash.

Berry picking is a favorite activity in the fertile Danubian Lowland.

Young and old alike flock to Slovakia's lakeside beaches during the summer months.

The rocky peaks and steep slopes of the Mala Fatra and the High Tatras challenge mountain climbers and hikers. Slovakia also boasts an extensive network of marked hiking trails. Boaters and canoeists enjoy the country's freshwater lakes and rivers. During the spring snowmelt, kayakers and canoeists carefully negotiate the rushing streams that flow down from the mountains of the north. Cyclists can trek along a bike trail that links Bratislava and Vienna, Austria.

Soccer remains Slovakia's most popular team sport. Bratislava is the home of many professional soccer teams, and amateur clubs play in many Slovakian cities and towns. Ice hockey is also popular among Slovaks during the winter. Bratislava and Kosice have the nation's top-rated hockey squads.

Slovak mountain climbers *(right)* brave the High Tatras. Soccer players *(below)* from Kosice celebrate their first-place win in an international tournament.

Using traditional plowing methods, farmers turn the soil of their small fields before planting. After decades of state control, most farms are now privately owned in post-Communist Slovakia.

# 4) The Economy

Before World War II, Slovakia was an agricultural region with limited heavy industry and manufacturing. But the postwar Communist regime transformed the country's economy. Heavy industry became the largest employer in Slovakia, where new factories produced industrial machinery, steel, and weapons.

By the late 1980s, however, the Czechoslovak economy was in poor shape. Under the central-planning system, many state-owned enterprises continued to make obsolete goods. With the fall of Communist regimes in central Europe, the market for armaments and other Slovak goods shrank even further. Factories closed or cut back production. In fact, declining living stan-

dards among factory workers played an important role in the overthrow of Communism in Czechoslovakia.

In the early 1990s, Czechoslovakia sold off many of its state-run firms through vouchers, which gave citizens the right to purchase shares in the companies. After the country's breakup in 1993, the Slovak government of Vladimir Meciar halted much of this privatization program. As a result, the pace of economic reform has been much slower in Slovakia than in the Czech Republic.

Fearing the unemployment that results when outdated businesses close, many Slovaks are opposed to privatization. They also resist foreign ownership of firms they work for and want wages, prices, and benefits under some form of government control. Unemployment in Slovakia remains high at 14 percent, and the average Slovak worker earns the equivalent of $182 a month.

Nevertheless, Slovakia has attracted investment from Austria, Germany, the Czech Republic, South Korea, and the United States. The economy began growing again in 1994 after many years of decline. Exports increased, and the rate of inflation (rising prices) slowed. The gradually improving economy encouraged those in the government who wished to continue the privatization program.

## Manufacturing

After World War II, the Communist government built new heavy industries and arms factories in Slovakia. A huge steel plant opened near Kosice, and Bratislava became the site of textile factories and oil refineries. Arms factories turned out tanks, artillery, and ammunition for Czechoslovakia's allies in the Warsaw Pact. By 1991 manufacturing accounted for about half of the nation's gross national product (GNP—the total value of all goods and services produced in the country).

The breakup of the Warsaw Pact in the early 1990s lessened tensions between Communist and non-Communist nations. As a result, the demand for arms quickly slowed, and more than four out of every five jobs in Slovakia's armaments industry disappeared. Although some weapons factories were converted to other uses, many are still unable to sell their goods on the international market.

In spite of these setbacks, 40 percent of the Slovak workforce still labors for manufacturing firms. Slovakia makes

Factory employees work as a team to blow, shape, and finish pieces of crystal for export.

Photo © John Eastcott/Yva Momatiuk

building materials, chemicals, cloth, iron, glass, footwear, and pharmaceuticals. In addition, some foreign manufacturing companies have invested in Slovakia, where wages are much lower than they are in western Europe. The German firm Volkswagen, for example, has opened an automobile plant, and Siemens, another German company, has invested in MEZ Michalovce, a Slovakian company that produces electric motors.

## Agriculture

For centuries Slovakia was a region of large farming estates, many of them owned by Hungarian nobles. In 1918, after the fall of Austria-Hungary, these lands were turned over to ethnic Slovaks. Nevertheless, many farmers moved to the cities in search of better-paying jobs. After World War II, this movement increased as the Communist government made large investments in heavy industry at the expense of the agricultural sector.

The Communist regime forced Slovak farmers to pool their land and machinery in cooperatives, which had to sell their produce at fixed prices. State farms, which the government owned and operated, were established on the largest properties. After the fall of Communism, the new Slovak government privatized most of the country's farmland.

Outdated farming machinery still brings in the harvest of the Danubian Lowland.

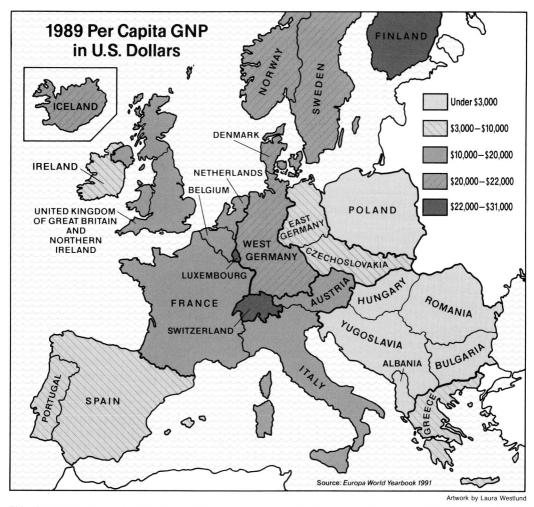

## 1989 Per Capita GNP in U.S. Dollars

| | |
|---|---|
| | Under $3,000 |
| | $3,000–$10,000 |
| | $10,000–$20,000 |
| | $20,000–$22,000 |
| | $22,000–$31,000 |

Source: *Europa World Yearbook 1991*

Artwork by Laura Westlund

This chart compares the average productivity per person—calculated by gross national product (GNP) per capita—for 26 European countries in 1989. The GNP is the value of all goods and services produced by a country in a year. In 1989, prior to achieving independence, Czechoslovakia had a per-capita GNP of $5,820, making it among the most economically sound eastern European nations. In 1993, after the two states separated, the per-capita GNP in Slovakia had dropped to $2,075, a figure that reflected its economic struggles. (In the same year, the Czech Republic's figure was $3,077.)

The nation's principal crops are rye, wheat, fruits, potatoes, and sugar beets. Livestock includes cattle, pigs, sheep, goats, and horses. The fertile Danubian Lowland is the most intensively farmed region, but farming remains a small part of the country's total output. Only 5 percent of Slovakia's GNP comes from agriculture, although more than 10 percent of the workforce is employed in this occupation.

## Mining and Energy

During its long history, Slovakia was an important center of silver and gold mining in central Europe. But by the twentieth century, miners had exhausted the nation's deposits of precious metals. Slovak mines now produce only small amounts of iron ore, copper, zinc, magnesite, and mercury. The construction industry uses Slovakia's limestone, gravel, and brick loam. Iron ore is the raw material for steelmaking, while

Slovnaft, a petroleum and petrochemical company headquartered in Bratislava, processes the crude oil that Slovakia buys from Russia. Half of the refined oil goes to the Czech Republic, but substantial amounts are also sold to Austria, Germany, Switzerland, Hungary, and Poland.

coal powers factories and electricity plants. The supply of many of these minerals does not meet demand, and Slovakia imports large amounts of both iron ore and coal.

Deposits of natural gas as well as a small petroleum field exist in the Danubian Lowland. Once able to import energy at low, fixed prices from the Soviet Union, Slovakia now must rely on its own production and on imported oil that it must buy at higher prices. A huge refinery near Bratislava processes the nation's imported crude oil.

Since it was built in the 1960s, the Jaslovske Bohunice nuclear power station has supplied more than half of Slovakia's electricity. To increase production, the Slovak government is building another nuclear power station at Mochovce.

Another major energy-producing project known as the Gabcikovo Dam was begun in the late 1980s. First planned by the Communist governments of Hungary and Czechoslovakia during the 1950s, this massive barrier across the Danube River is the largest civil engineering project in Europe. But by diverting water from the main channel of the Danube, the dam is draining the marshes that line the river and robbing cropland of needed irrigation water. Because of these environmental concerns, Hungary has refused to cooperate further in the project, throwing the future of the Gabcikovo Dam into doubt.

## Transportation and Tourism

An ancient center of trans-European trade, landlocked Slovakia now finds itself far from many of Europe's busiest transportation routes. After the fall of Communist governments in central Europe, the country began renovating its highway system. Main highways now link Bratislava with Budapest, Vienna, and Brno (in the Czech Republic). Outside of the main routes, however, many local roads are narrow and in need of repair.

Railways *(above)* link large cities, as well as smaller urban areas, throughout Slovakia. The country currently maintains about 2,000 miles of track. The ruggedness of Slovakia's terrain *(right)* has long made overland transportation difficult.

A paved highway twists and turns amid the forests of northern Slovakia.

A very important travel route in Slovakia is the Danube River, a principal shipping lane in central and eastern Europe. Bratislava—the busiest port in Slovakia—handles freighters and ferries that transport Slovak goods. Komarno, Slovakia's other major port, has shipyards that manufacture and repair cargo ships, tugs, dredgers, and ferries.

Slovakia has more than 2,000 miles of railway track, about half of which are electrified. Fast *rychlik* trains stop at large cities, while *osobny vlak* trains make all local stops. One important line runs between Bratislava and Sturovo, a town to the east on the Danube River, and then continues into Hungary.

Slovakia has five international airports. Stefanik Airport, the largest, handles regular commercial traffic between Bratislava and several foreign nations. The national airline of Czechoslovakia, CSA, survived the breakup of the country and still flies to the Middle East, North Africa, and North America.

Because the Communist government of Czechoslovakia strictly limited visits by foreigners, tourism was almost nonexistent in Slovakia for many years. But with its borders now open, Slovakia has become a popular vacation spot. The government is developing the transportation system and tourist facilities to attract travelers, who in turn bring in much-needed foreign income.

The High Tatras of the north provide opportunities for mountain climbing, hiking, and skiing. Slovakia also boasts glacial lakes, waterfalls, spas, underground caves, and five national parks. Ancient castles, many of them restored and open to the public, loom over the plains and river valleys. The cities of Kosice and Bratislava offer churches, palaces, and historic homes. Visitors to the old German cities of the Spis region and to the Rusyn villages of

Closed to foreigners for decades, Slovakia—and its many castles—are attracting visitors in large numbers. This old stronghold dominates a hill in Zvolen, a town south of Banska Bystrica.

the east can catch a glimpse of Slovakia's long and varied history.

## Foreign Trade

Under Communist rule, Slovakia conducted most of its foreign trade with other Communist nations in Europe. Slovak factories became an important source of armaments for the Warsaw Pact, but Slovakia had to import most of its fossil fuels, such as oil and natural gas, to keep its factories operating.

After the breakup of the Warsaw Pact, the Slovaks could no longer depend on trade with the former Communist-bloc nations. Instead, Slovakia had to compete in an open, international market. Slovak manufacturers found that many of their goods did not sell abroad. The result was a large trade deficit, meaning the country bought more goods than it could sell on the international market.

To solve this problem, Slovakia has increased taxes on goods imported from the Czech Republic, with which it conducts most of its foreign trade. But Slovakia has also signed the Central European Free Trade Agreement, a document that will one day establish a free-trade zone among Hungary, Poland, the Czech Republic, and Slovakia. As a result, trade policy has become an important issue between the governments of Slovakia and the Czech Republic.

The Czech Republic remains Slovakia's biggest trading partner, accounting for

Photo © John Eastcott/Yva Momatiuk

Because of some economic reforms, the country's earliest ironworks is now able to charge market prices for its steel and pipes.

Photo by Andrzej Polec

Every July thousands of pilgrims, both from Slovakia and from foreign countries, arrive at Levoca's cathedral for a religious festival. Centuries ago a Hungarian king gave Levoca a special commercial status, which allowed the city to prosper as a major trading hub from the thirteenth to the seventeenth centuries. In fact, the town still has many buildings that date from its wealthy past.

42 percent of Slovakia's exports and 36 percent of its imports. Germany, Russia, Hungary, and Austria also buy and sell goods in Slovakia. Imports include transportation equipment, machinery, fuels, and chemicals. Slovakia exports machinery, building materials, food, and transportation equipment.

## The Future

Slovakia's independence has brought new problems and challenges. The nation now competes for trade and foreign investment with the Czech Republic and with other, fast-developing neighbors. Slovakia's economy remains weak, and the loss of foreign markets has forced many of its businesses to close. In addition, the nation's leaders are sharply divided about how to prepare for the future. Although Vladimir Meciar faces strong opposition, even within his own party, a leader of equal popularity has not yet emerged to challenge him.

In addition, Slovakia is experiencing tension among its various ethnic groups. Some Slovaks believe that ethnic Hungarians seek further self-rule—perhaps even independence—from the Slovak government. The issue has caused friction between the Slovak and Hungarian governments. But prosperity from a growing tourism sector, bigger crop harvests, and more open trade in central Europe may help Slovakia to overcome its social and political problems.

# Index

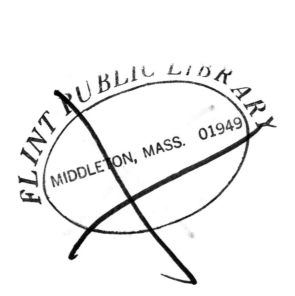